194

TONIA TODMAN'S
Stencilling
BOOK

First published in 1992 by
Sally Milner Publishing
558 Darling Street
Rozelle NSW 2039
Australia

Reprinted 1992

© Todman Services Pty Ltd, 1992

Production by Sylvana Scannapiego, ·
Island Graphics
Design by Gatya Kelly
Layout by Shirley Peters
Photography by Andrew Elton
Illustrations by Angela Downes
Typeset by Shirley Peters
Printed in Malaysia by SRM Production Services

National Library of Australia
Cataloguing-in-Publication data:

Todman, Tonia.
    Tonia Todman's stencilling book.

    ISBN 1 86351 098 2

    1. Stencil work I. Title. II. Title: Stencilling book.

745.73

Contents

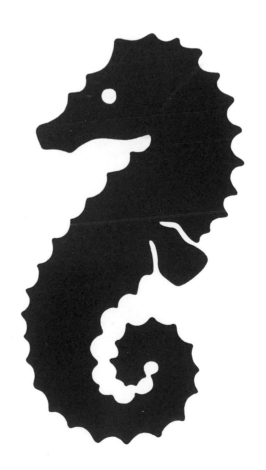

Introduction

Stencilling has been used to decorate homes for a very long time. Back in the depths of history the first stenciller pressed their hand to the damp wall of a cave and blew clay dust around it, leaving a perfect impression for us to find many, many years later! From that moment, it seems, the art of stencilling started. It did not take long for that not-so-artistic home decorator to realise that stencilling was a very adaptable way of personalising his or her home, and that these creative transformations came about very quickly.

Vastly refined, explored and adapted, the technique of stencilling remains one of the few truly unique aspects of home decorating. All the choices are yours – what design you choose, where you stencil, what colours you select, what paints you use and how you apply them are all open to your judgement. You can really achieve a totally exclusive effect – and what's more – it's incredibly inexpensive and easy!

Throughout the book is a large selection of varied stencils, which includes, I hope, something for everyone. Use them just as they are, use part of a design, or mix them together, or increase or decrease their size according to your needs.

So gather up the few tools needed, and start that stencilled transformation somewhere in your home. All you need to know is contained in the following pages. Stencilling is one of my favourite crafts, but I must warn you that it is known to be addictive. Good results are so commonplace that soon you will be seeing stencilling opportunities everywhere!

Materials and equipment

Manilla cardboard

Acquire medium weight card, available from stationers, or recycle discarded office files. Your design must fit within 2 cm (1″) of the card edges. If your design is larger than your card, butt two sheets of card together and fasten with one strip of overlapping masking tape on each side, completely covering the butted edges. Manilla card is the traditional card for stencils and in earlier times was really the only choice, other than thin tin plating, for the home stenciller. This card is an alternative to acetate sheeting.

Linseed oil and turpentine mixture

Pour a mixture of 50 per cent linseed oil and 50 per cent turpentine into a jar with a screw-on lid, and shake well. Label the jar clearly. This mixture will be used to waterproof the manilla cardboard. You'll also need soft cloths to apply it.

Mylar™ plastic

These sheets of 'plastic' are really acetate, and are strong, clear and very durable. Choose the thicker gauges if you have the option. No-longer required X-rays are wonderful, as they come in such large sheets, and are of high quality. See page 7 for a comparison of the qualities of card and acetate stencils.

Cutting board

There is an amazing product called a self-healing cutting board. It is a much loved tool of patchworkers, who use it when cutting fabrics with a rotary cutter. The same board is ideal for cutting stencils, as it has the ability to self-heal any cut made in it, even after prolonged use. They are usually dark green in colour, and are painted in various measured grids and angles which are of some use for aligning the stencil while cutting. Alternatively, cut your stencils on a thick sheet of glass. Either have the edges of the glass rounded off, or wrap them in masking tape. Glass has the advantage of transparency, which means you can place a design under the glass and, if using acetate for stencils, trace the design onto the acetate in one step. Another cutting surface can be provided by several layers of newspapers, or simply cut onto an old breadboard.

Craft knife

You may have access to a scalpel, which is ideal, or purchase a craft knife with replaceable blades from a hardware or art supply shop. Whichever you use, the point must be sharp and the handle easily gripped. Some stationers sell small cutters designed to cut sections from papers and magazines. These have a small, sharp push-out blade and work well for the life of the non-replaceable blade.

Cartridge paper, soft and hard lead pencils, ruler and tape measure, eraser, chalk, tracing paper and felt–tipped pens

All are available from stationers and are necessary for drawing and transferring designs. You'll need chalk when positioning stencils on large objects or walls. A tape measure is needed to give you precise horizontal and vertical starting points; the chalk is used to mark these points, and is easily wiped away later with a damp cloth.

Masking tape

Needed for holding stencils in place while painting, or for masking off nearby areas of the stencil when another colour is being applied. Ideal too for mending accidents, such as cutting through a bridge or section not intended for such treatment!

Spray adhesive

I personally do not enjoy using this product as its smell bothers me and it can cause skin irritations. However, I know professional stencillers who cannot work without it, as it allows them to position stencils wherever needed without fiddling with masking tape. Simply spray the back of the stencil with the adhesive and wait a few

seconds before pressing it into position. It can usually be repositioned over and over again without applying more glue, and does not seem to leave any residue after the stencil is removed. It does give a completely flat bond of stencil to surface, and this overcomes the occasional problem of vertical paint seepage under stencils while working on walls.

Paints

I suggest that stencillers use acrylic paints, rather than oil based paints. Oil based paints are not unsuitable, just more difficult to use and clean up. I have found it more difficult to achieve subtle effects with oil paints, as you usually have to have them fairly liquid to go on smoothly. Too much liquid in stencil paints is disastrous. If collecting basic acrylic colours, I suggest you purchase red, navy blue, bright yellow, white and black. These are only the basics, and further additions will certainly follow; your art supplies outlet can advise you on these purchases. I discuss colour schemes and the theory of colour mixing later in the book. Oil paints can be sprayed on from spray cans, but again, I caution beginners. Spray paint drifts and oil paints are difficult to remove. See notes later about the use of spray paints in the section headed *Painting Techniques and Colour Schemes.*

Stencil Crayons

These are really compressed, dry oil paints in a crayon shape. Thay have a smooth, somewhat oily texture, and resemble pressed face powder. These crayons are wonderful for beginners, as they do not require water, and, as such, mean that no blurred stencil edges will be caused by excess water on the brush or sponge. Include them amongst your basic equipment, as they provide a very different finish to that of paints. For information on how to use them, see the section headed *Painting Techniques and Colour Schemes.*

Brushes

Brushes that have their bristles cut straight across, rather than coming to a point, are suitable as stencil brushes. These are essential as paint is applied in a dabbing motion, sometimes called pouncing, not stroked on. Brushes can be round or oblong shaped, with long, or short stubby handles. I prefer to have a variety of sizes, and like to have one for each colour I use in a stencil. Cost is a consideration, and like everything in this world, quality is usually expensive. Bristle brushes come in various price ranges, and are very suitable. Synthetic bristles are also suitable, but may not last as long as genuine bristle brushes. I have often purchased a normal, thick, inexpensive brush and carefully trimmed the bristles flat myself, using sharp scissors. Some normal, thick brushes have tips that are not quite flat, yet they seem to stencil quite well. Also, very small, oblong or 'flattened' brushes are a good idea to have in your collection. They usually have flat, or near-flat tips, and are very good for stencilling narrow stems and small areas.

Sponges

The application of paint through the stencil using a small natural sponge is an exciting technique. The resulting effect is charmingly uneven, and the application of paint is as quick, if not quicker, than when using a brush. Do not use synthetic sponge, as its surface is too regular and the painted effect is not very attractive.

Paper towels, paint trays, water containers

Recycle containers and jars for paint trays and water containers. If paper towel is out of the question, use old, absorbent scrap fabric.

Compass

Use a compass if you wish to design a geometric motif involving circular lines. Don't try to draw these lines freehand unless your intention is for the motif to have a traditional country feel that does not demand accuracy.

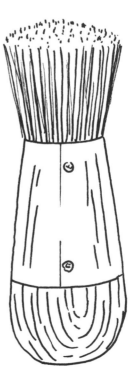

Brushes with flat-cut bristles are ideal for stencilling

Designing and cutting a stencil

What is a stencil?

Think of a stencil as a sheet of cardboard or plastic which has had a pattern cut from its centre. This sheet – or stencil – is placed onto the object to be decorated and paint is applied through the design, using either a traditional stencil brush, a small natural sponge, or spray paint from a can. When the stencil is lifted the painted design remains on the surface beneath. As stencils are enduring, you can re-position the stencil and duplicate the design as many times as you wish.

Stencil designs may be complex, using a series of different stencils to create separate parts of the design in different colours. This is standard procedure for traditional stencilling, where the scale and complexity of stencilled designs was usually rather grand! For information on making and using multi-part stencils see page 9. Designs of one colour only can be simply charming, and when used imaginatively are highly effective decorative elements. You will find all the stencil designs in this book are single-part stencils that lend themselves to using one or more colours. I suggest beginners start with simple shapes cut from a single stencil, and consider using one or two colours only in the design.

What designs are good for stencils?

The answer to this is simple – just about any design is suitable to be worked on and cut into a stencil. Very small, closely spaced designs will prove difficult, unless they are all in one colour, and large flowing designs are best handled by more experienced stencillers, not because they are technically difficult, but the positioning of the stencil needs an experienced eye.

I like to be inspired by the designs around me. Perhaps the fabric on your sofa has a design you could adapt to stencil onto nearby lampshades, the design in the feature tiles in your kitchen or bathroom could be adapted to stencil onto curtain or blind fabric, or maybe your timber floor needs the definition of a border influenced by a nearby lead-light or etched window pattern.

Providing you observe the following notes about adequate bridges and well defined windows in your stencils, any design is possible. There are many stencil patterns illustrated in this book and, if you are a beginner, you may like to start with the techniques of stencilling, and leave designing your own stencil until next time!

Which to use as a stencil base – cardboard or acetate?

Stencils can be cut from either oil-coated Manilla cardboard, or high quality acetate sheeting. Both have their advantages, with the main concerns being cost and availability. Manilla cardboard is by far the cheapest material, and the most readily available. Stencils cut from acetate will last longer than cardboard stencils, though these sheets may be harder to find, and will cost more than cardboard. Drawing your design onto acetate is quick and easy, as you are able to trace through the transparent plastic, eliminating the tracing steps needed for cardboard stencils. However, sometimes the oiled board is so translucent that you can place it over your design and trace as if you were using plastic sheeting. You may be able to make yourself a primitive light-box. Place a sheet of glass propped up so that light is behind it. You may need to position a desk lamp so that it provides the direct light onto the back of the glass. When you place the stencil outline onto the glass with stencil card over it, you can see the outline of the design quite clearly, and therefore trace straight onto the card. The stencils illustrated in the book are solid black and will show up well on a light-box.

How to plan and design a stencil

It is quite natural to look at a stencil and be somewhat confused! Even the experienced stenciller needs to look carefully to be clear about the elements in the design. Even then it is often not until you are cross-hatching the areas to be cut out that you may see a section that won't work. What you see when you look at a cut-out stencil are spaces called 'windows', and the bits connecting these spaces to each other and to the background are called 'bridges'. The windows and the bridges together make up the design. Windows are simple – they are the spaces through which the paint is applied. The bridges serve two purposes. They give strength to the stencil, holding the cut-out windows in place, and they are also a design element. They can merely be the borders between two areas of colour with no distinct design contribution, or they can be truly important to the design, bringing distinct lines and shapes to the overall pattern. Whatever their purpose, bridges should not be obvious. They should blend in with the flow of the design, for example, if your design is curved, the larger bridges should also be curved. In a geometic pattern, the bridges are usually an integral part of the design. Without them there would be no pattern, as these narrow, regularly shaped bridges actually create the geometric pattern.

Practise first on paper. Draw or trace shapes that please you, perhaps repeating these motifs to form borders. Traditional Victorian, art deco or folk art motifs abound in books, and are wonderful bases for a design. If you haven't drawn and cut stencils before, make them as simple as a row of stars and half moons, or a flower and leaf design. Now, using your drawing pen or pencil, block in the window areas with crisscrossed lines. You will then see where to cut away, how the bridges will work, and whether the design will 'stay together' when you cut, as it will if the bridges are adequately sized and spaced.

Compare the two drawings. One is the original sketch, the other is the same sketch modified to become a stencil with the inclusion of bridges

Designing and drawing a multi-part stencil

A multi-part stencil is just as it sounds, in that there are several separate stencil sheets needed to complete the design. The overall effect of these designs is somewhat different to traditional stencilling, and you tend to get a 'painted' look to your work. If you look closely at some designs or stencils you may see spots where there is no bridging around some areas, and where colours butt right up to, or overlap each other. These are multi-part stencils, and a brief definition describes them as a stencil for each colour, each being painted in successive order until the design is complete. For example, let's assume you wish to stencil a strawberry. A strawberry has a red body, black spots on the red body, and a green leafy top. The black spots overlap the red body, and the green leafy part butts up to the red body with no bridges in between. The design is drawn identically three times (once for each colour) each on its own plastic stencil sheet. On the first sheet, cut out only the red body. On the second, cut out only the black spots, and on the third, cut out only the green leafy top. Lay down the red body first and stencil. Overlay the black spots, aligning the edge of the red body with the drawn lines in the stencil, and stencil the dots onto the red body. Do the same with the green leafy top, stencilling the leaves that will butt up to the red body. It is important that paint layers are dry before proceeding to the next colour.

This is a very simple example, and you can imagine how complex and time consuming the process can become. Multi-part stencils are not recommended for beginners. However it is a stencilling skill to strive for, and one that can be very satisfying.

A simple example of the steps in cutting a multi-part stencil. The shaded areas were each cut from a separate stencil. Re-draw the full design each time to assist you with re-aligment

Enlarging or decreasing a design

The traditional, time consuming way of making a design bigger (scaled up) is to draw a grid of evenly spaced lines over the design. Draw a larger grid with the same number of lines and copy the design, square by square, onto the larger grid. This can be reversed by re-drawing the design onto a smaller grid, thus reducing the size of the design. This can be an accurate and also inexpensive method of re-scaling any design.

Another way, and by far the simplest, quickest and most accurate method is to use the enlarging or decreasing facility of a photostat machine. You may have to piece the resulting sections of a large design together to get your complete design.

All the designs I've included in this book are suitable to be enlarged or decreased, though you should be careful the bridges do not become too small and unstable if the design is made smaller. You may have to adjust these later when cutting the stencil.

Oiling cardboard

This process is done before any drawing or cutting of stencils is started. The Manilla card will become slightly translucent, stronger and more pliable, and waterproof. I like to make up a 50/50 linseed oil and turpentine mixture in a screw-top jar and shake it to blend.

Apply the mixture with a cloth to both sides of the cardboard. Rub in well but gently until the card is saturated. Pin the card up to dry for half an hour or so. Wipe away excess oiliness with a soft cloth. Dampen cloths with water when finished, then dispose of them as spontaneous combustion can occur if the oily cloths are stored.

Tracing and transferring onto oiled cardboard

Place a sheet of tracing paper over a design and, using a pencil, trace the design. If the design is simply the base motif, and it has yet to be worked into the windows and bridges stage, trace off this motif and re-work the design on tracing paper, placing bridges where necessary and then cross-hatching the window areas. You may need to re-trace the completed design again to obtain a 'clean' copy. On the reverse side of the traced design, draw over the design thickly with a soft lead pencil. Turn the tracing paper right side up and centre it over your oiled board, and rub gently on the pencil outline with the blunt end of the pencil. Remove the tracing paper and draw around the faint outline which has appeared. Cross-hatch the window areas again – just to prevent any confusion!

Sometimes, as I discussed earlier, the oiled cardboard becomes so translucent that you can trace through it. Simply place your clearly outlined motif underneath the cardboard and draw around it with a soft lead pencil. This process is helped enormously by using a 'light-box'.

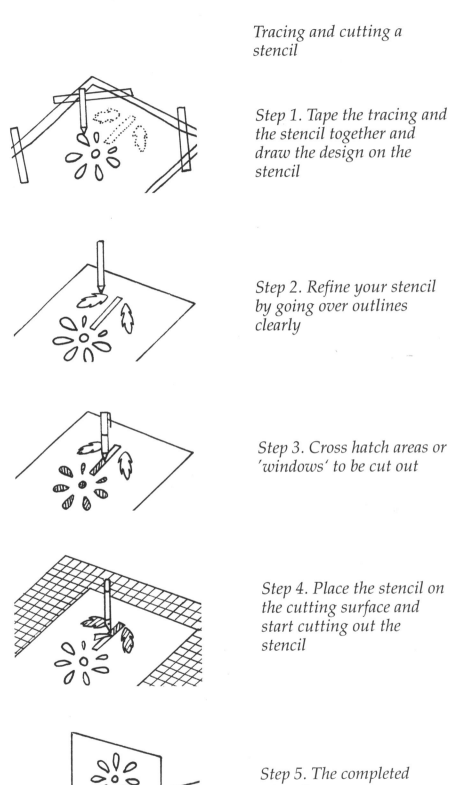

Tracing and cutting a stencil

Step 1. Tape the tracing and the stencil together and draw the design on the stencil

Step 2. Refine your stencil by going over outlines clearly

Step 3. Cross hatch areas or 'windows' to be cut out

Step 4. Place the stencil on the cutting surface and start cutting out the stencil

Step 5. The completed stencil

Transferring a design onto acetate

This is one of the simplest steps of all. Create your design, complete with accurate window areas and bridges, following instructions in the previous step. To make an acetate stencil you need only a clear outline on your completed design. Centre the sheet of acetate over the design and draw in the outlines with a felt-tipped pen. Cross-hatching the window areas on the acetate will make things clearer for you.

Cutting a stencil from cardboard or acetate

Place the stencil card or acetate on your cutting surface and using a sharp craft knife or scalpel, start cutting from the middle of the design, so that you are not working over previously cut areas and risking damage to the delicate bridges. Try to cut away small windows first. Always cut towards you, rotating the stencil as you go and keeping a firm and even cutting pressure on your work. Try to cut so that your wrist does most of the work, rather than your shoulder and elbow too, as this will only make you tired. It will take you time to become accustomed to the action needed! You may feel you are very slow at first, and no doubt you will be cautious, but in time you will be cutting stencils with speed and enthusiasm.

Drawing and cutting a repetitive border stencil

Borders are designed with motifs which are repeated regularly. Most border stencils are designs that are simply repeated over and over again, giving an unbroken sequence. If you place one end of a border stencil to overlap the other end, the designs should match exactly. Decide on your design; follow the various steps of drawing, tracing and transferring. Draw the design onto cardboard or acetate, leaving a minimum of 15 cm (6") blank at one end. You should have at least one section of the design repeated. Let's say, for example, that your basic border design was one large flower followed by three smaller flowers. Cut out the design starting with one large flower, then cut the three small flowers, then repeat the large flower motif again. Follow the last large flower with the blank area. Bend the card to have the ends overlap, with the cut-out end on top. Overlap the large flowers evenly, and then, drawing through the cut out small flowers, copy their outlines onto the blank end of the stencil. Cut out these small flowers. This form of duplication ensures continuity of the design with absolutely accurate spacing and sizing of the motifs.

Use the repeated motifs as a positioning guide when painting a border. Simply overlap and align the motifs at the end of the stencil card with the ones just painted and your stencil is ready to use again.

Another trick to make things easier is to actually cut motifs at the required distance from the stencil edge that you will be needing them. Whatever does she mean,

A repetitive border showing duplicated motifs ready to be cut. Use these duplicated motifs to help you align the border

you may well ask! If, for example, you are stencilling around under your ceiling cornice, and you wish the stencil to be 2 cm (1") from the lower lip of the cornice, position your design on the card so that the top edge of the motif is 2 cm (1") from the edge of the stencil, then, when stencilling, you merely have to push the card firmly up to meet the cornice lip and your alignment is accurate.

Repairs and joins in stencils

It is inevitable that mistakes and accidents will happen during cutting – even experienced stencillers have this problem! Before you despair and start all over again, see if you can work your way around it, perhaps by incorporating the cut space into some other design element. It's amazing how easily an unintentional window can become another flower or leaf with a little extra cutting. If this is not possible, try layering the area with strips of masking tape, top and bottom, then re-cut. This method can also be used to mend broken bridges, or repair a well-used stencil.

Care of your stencils

Whether you use acetate or cardboard stencils, wipe them over after use to prevent build-up of dried paint around the edges of the windows. If necessary, acetate stencils can be immersed in warm water and washed with soap and a slightly abrasive brush or cloth to remove dried paint. This is not usually a suitable treatment for cardboard stencils, so you will have to wipe away excess paint frequently during use, using a damp cloth or sponge. I should add that it is surprising how resilient cardboard stencils can be. Once, in desperation, I actually rubbed away dried paint from a neglected stencil using a soapy kitchen pot scrubber and the paint came away leaving the stencil unharmed. Card stencils can build up paint around their window edges, and this can be pared away carefully with your craft knife when the stencil and paint are dry. If paint is allowed to build up, small areas can sometimes disappear, and larger areas become distorted.

Dry all stencils thoroughly after use, and store them flat, perhaps layering your original drawings with the stencil for later reference.

Positioning stencils

Spacing borders

Borders provide some of the most interesting stencil effects, and I love using them. They are so very dramatic and decisive; they can provide the definitive edge to paintwork, emphasise ceilings, chair rails or floor areas in the house, and provide a myriad of decorative possibilities when combined with accessories. Borders can be a simple repetition of the same motif using only one colour, or can actually show a complex scene with a combination of motifs and colours.

Some mathematical calculations are needed if you wish to stencil a border that does not lend itself well to wrapping around a corner. You will have to measure the total length of the motif, from repeat to repeat – that is, say, from the beginning of the large flower to the beginning of the next large flower. Arrange multiples of this distance along your wall to decide just how many motifs you will be able to stencil along it. Chances are that you will not fit them evenly, so you then have to plan how much space you need to leave between them. It's easier than it sounds! Remember that the human eye will notice a jumble before it notices spaciousness, so don't be tempted to cram the motifs if they don't fit evenly.

Once you know how much space you need to leave, take a piece of chalk and mark the outline of the beginning motif along the wall, marking through the stencil outline to be accurate. It's simply a matter of then stencilling along the wall, moving from chalk-mark to chalk-mark and aligning the stencil for accurate spacing.

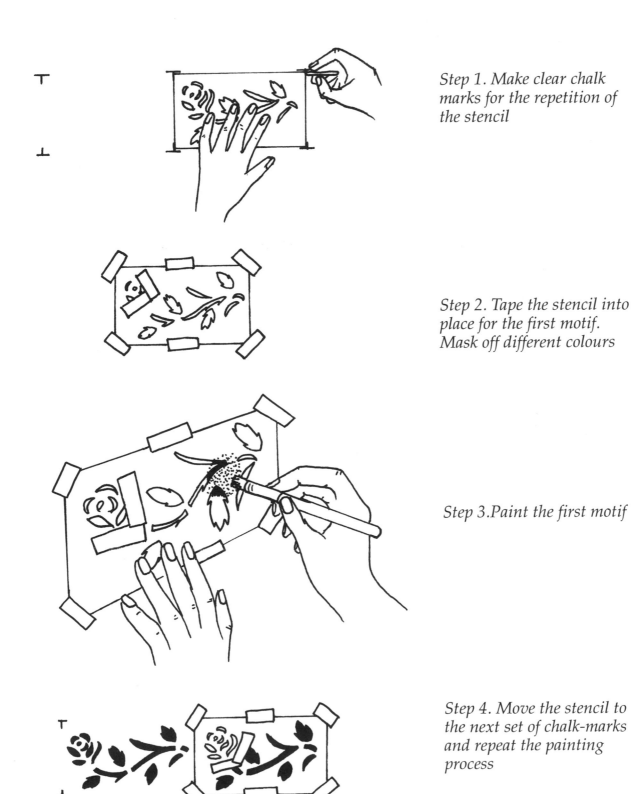

Step 1. Make clear chalk marks for the repetition of the stencil

Step 2. Tape the stencil into place for the first motif. Mask off different colours

Step 3.Paint the first motif

Step 4. Move the stencil to the next set of chalk-marks and repeat the painting process

Spacing single motifs

Single motifs work in the same spacing manner as borders. You need to do some calculations to determine the distance between each motif, and the simplest way is to chalk-mark the wall or item with these positions. Preliminary accuracy is a sure way to enjoyable stencilling! Remove the chalk-mark later with a damp cloth.

To stencil a pattern in the centre of an item, a ruler and chalk are indispensable. Mark horizontal and vertical lines on the stencil with chalk to find its centre, and do the same on the item to be stencilled. Align these centre points and tape the stencil into position with masking tape.

Corners

Inside corners provide the most challenge to stencillers. An effective corner treatment when using a border is to end the border short of the corner and then stencil a larger motif, which not only complements the border pattern, but creates a feature. The Victorians used this design ploy to great advantage, with beautiful borders ending with a pair of grand motifs that wrapped into and around the corner and provided a start for the border again on the next wall. This still works well today, and you can easily design simple motifs to start and finish your borders. If you're interested, study books that detail Victorian designs, for more traditional inspiration. They were masters of spacing and design, and while they were fond of complexity and ornamentation, there is still plenty to learn from their well-documented ideas.

You can also cut a new stencil and cut through it at precisely the corner. Butt the cut edges together at the corner and stencil the design.

The other way, much cruder by far, of stencilling into and around an inside corner is to simply push your stencil into the corner and stencil as fast as possible so that your stencil does not become permanently bent!

Entirely possible though it may be, this method tends to give indistinct outlines and very often draws attention to the corner. If you are left with no choice, tape your stencil into place without actually forcing a crease at the corner. If you do this gently, and stencil into the corner with great care, you may well get a good result.

Outside corners are much simpler. Stencil right up to the corner, then lift your stencil – do not just wrap it around the corner. Re-position the stencil on the other side of the corner, matching the motif where you left off. It is not difficult, and the eye will scarcely notice any small inaccuracies. Sometimes it may be necessary to take a fine paint brush and paint in some connecting lines if the corner is slightly rounded. This often happens in older houses where the corners are not precise right angles.

Curves

If you sew, you will know how it is possible to make evenly spaced cuts in a piece of straight paper from one side almost to the other side, then to fan out these cuts to create a curved shape on the cut side. This is a technique often used in pattern making. While the process of making curved border stencils is tedious, the results are wonderful. Draw your design onto a piece of paper, then cut into it from the side which will be opened out. Fan out your design around the curve to be stencilled. Tape it in place around the curve, then trace over it to see how much you will have to fill in to make the design curve while still making the motifs recognisable. My experience here tells me that it is best to have a repeated small motif, say 3 to 4 cm (1$^1/_2$") wide that you can cut between. Then the design is not disrupted by cuts, and will not need extensive redrawing.

Other tips

If your stencil design travels around a small box, for example, overlaps just don't seem to matter. Start at what may be the back of the box, or a corner, and continue around until the design overlaps or butts. The start and finish is usually less noticable than you would expect. If you were stencilling a heart-shaped box, start and finish in the upper inside corner, not the lower point.

If repeating a single motif around a circle, first make a paper template of the circle. Fold the circle in half, in half again, then continue folding until you have several even divisions – similar to the segments in a cut orange. These divisions will help you space your motif accurately around the circle. Put the template back onto the circle and mark with chalk the dividing lines which give the motif positions.

Effective places and things to stencil

Before the advent of wallpaper, stencilled walls were quite common in most houses. In many Western countries, professional stencillers would travel around the countryside offering their decorating services, often cutting special stencils to meet with the approval of the householder. The availability of printed wallpaper brought this craft to a fairly rapid standstill during the 1930s. The home, generally, and the accessories we surround ourselves with are now the main focus of stencillers. Following are some suggested items, or areas, that I know to be effective for stencilling.

Walls

These still provide the largest, most versatile, area for stencilling. All-over small patterns, even just a sprig of flowers or leaves are very attractive, as are friezes near cornices and chair rails. Taking a border around a wall

above a skirting rail and continuing it around door and window frames can be very effective.

Behind plates and pictures

A stencilled bow on the wall just above a picture or a plate can 'frame' them attractively.

Picture frames

A rope design, or something similar, can look wonderful when stencilled on a picture or mirror frame on a flat area of the moulding.

Lampshades

Simple stencils on plain lampshades can successfully link room accessories together.

Table and bed linen

Stencilled tablecloths, placemats and napkins look wonderful, as do pillowcases and sheet fold-backs.

Trays

Stencil a tray to match your favourite china.

Floors

Borders on floors define edges and dining areas effectively. Canvas floor 'cloths' or rugs were extensively used in Victorian times, and these can still be effective today. They need to be made from a substantial fabric such as cotton sailcloth or canvas, and are later given several coats of acrylic varnish to seal and preserve the pattern. The sealing also gives the rug necessary stiffness and resilience.

Fabric

Stencilling gives an opportunity to create your own furnishing fabric. Pure cotton and linen are the best base cloths, and if you are planning to launder it rather than dryclean it later, wash it first to remove any starch or dressing. Iron it smooth prior to stencilling. Stencil onto fabric using fabric paints, or acrylic paints with a fabric medium added. Your paint supplier will advise you about these paints. Fabric can be stencilled with random patterns, borders, or geometric designs. If a whole curtain length seems too much for you, perhaps you

could start with sufficient fabric for some cushions. Fabric paints need to be heat-sealed, and this is best done by ironing the stencilled fabric on the wrong side with a medium-heat iron.

Ceramics

This could be an easy way to transform an unattractive bathroom. There are ceramic paints available which are especially made for bathroom conditions. These dry slowly, and need sealing, but are most effective. Your craft paint supplier can advise you further.

Furniture

Stencils have long been used to emphasise the shape and design of tables, dressers and chairs. Woven cane items can look very pretty when stencilled.

Clothing

Personalise your own clothing with stencilling. A shirt can look wonderful if it's stencilled in some way, or simply stencil a square of fabric to create a scarf.

Household accessories

The list of possibilities here is endless. Virtually any flat or slightly curved surface is a potential stencil base. Often the most drab item can be completely transformed with some stencilling. Frequent junk shop forays can result in all sorts of treasure that's just right for stencilling!

Painting techniques and colour schemes

Stencilling with a brush

Fix your stencil in place with little strips of masking tape. Be sure it is flat against the object you are stencilling. Spread a little acrylic paint (about enough to cover a thumbnail) onto your paint tray. I am still fascinated that so little paint is used in stencilling! Dab the dry brush onto the paint to load it, stroking away excess. Then dab the brush onto kitchen towel to remove any excess paint. Paint is applied through the stencil windows with an up and down dabbing motion. Do not stroke your paint onto the stencil, as this only pushes paint under the edges and gives an indistinct outline. Excess moisture in your brush, or in your paints, will cause problems as very moist paint will seep under the stencil and blur edges, or if stencilling vertically, drip downwards.

Colour builds up gradually under your control, and you will learn to create soft or strong effects by graduating the amount of colour applied. Do not aim to have every section filled with an identical amount of paint. One of the charming visual aspects of stencilling is the overall uneven effect of the colour.

Try to paint the larger areas first; start in the centre of the window and work towards the edges. You may like to add more colour in places, to simulate shadow, or paint the area lightly to show light reflection. Try applying paint only around the edges of large windows. This can give an interesting light and shade effect.

Try to keep one brush for each colour you use. If this is not possible, at least keep one for dark colours, and another for light colours.

When cleaning a brush, remove paint thoroughly with pure soap and cool water. Squeeze the bristles firmly between a towel to remove moisture, then re-shape them to their original shape and, if possible, allow to dry before using. If you have to use a brush while it's damp – and this will happen – be very sure you have squeezed as much moisture as possible from the brush. Do not push the bristles out in a daisy shape against a towel to dry the centre, however tempting it may be!

Stencilling with a natural sponge

Many of the methods for sponge painting are the same as brush methods. Sponges last a long time, and are generally less expensive than good stencil brushes. Because sponges are much larger than brushes, applying paint with a sponge tends to be quicker than with brushes. However, painting small areas can be a little tricky as you cannot see what you are doing! Select a small, well-shaped natural sponge, not one with odd-shaped bits protruding from it. Try to see that the holes are fairly even, too, as large holes or indentations will give an unattractive effect. This is asking a lot of a natural product, and you may find a sponge with one side only that has all the qualities you need!

To paint with a sponge, you will first need to dampen the sponge, and squeeze it out thoroughly in a towel. You really only want to change it from being rigid, as it is when totally dry, to being soft and pliable. Pressing it dry between layers of a towel will reduce moisture content to a minimum. Apply paint as for brushes, using the same dabbing technique. Ideally, you should have several sponges, keeping one for each colour, or at least one for light colours, another for dark. Sponges come clean in pure soap and cool water. Rinse them well, squeeze out excess moisture and allow to dry. You may like to wear close-fitting rubber gloves while applying paint with a sponge, and thus avoid dried paint under your fingernails!

Spray painting a stencil

Some experts in this technique describe it as the easiest method of applying paint to stencils. I can understand their enthusiasm, as it is super-quick and gives lovely, hazy paint effects. However, I find that the biggest problem with spray painting is the amount of paint you get where you don't want it. Spray paint drifts, and no matter how cautious you are, some always seems to land inconveniently in the most obvious place! Given this warning, if you are able to shield surrounding areas, and the remainder of the object beyond the edge of the stencil, then you should try it.

Firmly tape down the edges of the stencil with masking tape, and cover the other areas, especially the floor, with sheets of newspaper, and try to work in a still room – no breezes coming through open windows, please! Always wear a face mask, as the fumes from paint at close quarters are unpleasant. Practise using the spray can – there is ample paint in a spray can for you to do many practice runs on paper – and concentrate on the pressure you apply to the press-button. You have to be able to control the press-button evenly and lightly. Heavy bursts of paint will only run under the stencil edges. Try to achieve a light, hazy effect, not unlike expert stippling, and try moving the can in gentle arcs as you paint.

The colours available in spray paints are fairly limited, compared with those in tubed acrylic paints. Investigate those spray paints available for automotive repairs. The nozzles on these cans seem to be more substantial, making the paint flow easier to control, and the colours available are more varied and vibrant.

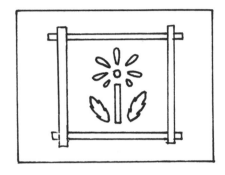

Step 1. Mask off area around stencil and tape securely

Step 2. Spray directly onto stencil

Stencilling with stencil crayons

Rub a little crayon onto a blank section of the stencil, or rub some onto aluminium foil. Take a dry stencil brush and rub it into your crayon markings, using a circular motion. This will load the brush with crayon colour. Using gentle circular motions, wipe the brush very lightly across the stencil in the sections to be coloured, leaving a faint colour print. Now re-load your brush, and go over these areas again, still using circular motions and building up more colour, concentrating on the edges of the cut-outs, rather than the middle.

Crayons give a much more subtle colour effect than paints. It is possible to create very delicate effects of light and shade, and variable colour effects can be created by loading different coloured crayons onto your brush at the same time. Ideally a separate brush should be used for each crayon colour, but if this is not possible you should clean your brushes with mineral turpentine then wash them in pure soap and warm water before using another colour. I suggest you try holding a curved piece of paper over the centre of a leaf design, allowing you to stencil a veined effect. This method can also be used when stencilling with paints.

Crayons are not recommended for stencilling on fabrics that will be used and laundered often, but are ideal for wall stencilling, or any vertical stencilling, as the lack of water in their application makes the whole stencilling process quicker and cleaner. It means you can ascend a ladder without having to juggle wet paints, and therefore eliminate the all-important drop-sheets protecting the floors!

Stencilled cupboard

Roses

Stencilled memories

The seaside at your feet

Nursery Magic

Stencilled writing paper and envelopes

A Victorian-inspired floor stencil

Schoolhouse quilt

Embroidered stencil on a silk cushion

Over-painting with several colours

You may have seen professionally done stencilling in which areas appear to have several colours blended. This is called over-painting. It is an interesting technique to try, especially in more complex stencils, as it gives great depth and shape to your motifs. Once you have tried it you will really notice the difference between flat, one-coloured stencils, and over-painted stencils. Colours can be heightened by the laying of several shades of the one colour, or two colours can be built up to create a third. The method requires practice, though it is not difficult. It is only through experience that you will understand the amounts of paint to lay on, the results of colour combining, and the effects of creating light and shade in a motif.

Let's say you wish to stencil a simple bow. Rather than have it appear in a flat pink colour, you decide to add two other shades of pink, one lighter, one darker. Using any of the three paint application methods, stencil the bow in the medium pink. Then start to apply the darker paint. The bow will have shadows around the knot, and perhaps down the tails, and certainly in amongst the loops. The highlights would be at the top of the knot, the top and some surface areas of the loops, and some on the tails and the tail tips. These extra shades are stencilled in the normal way, using a light hand, and cautious application of colour. Fruit and flower shapes seem to respond very well to over-painting. I prefer to use a dry sponge when over-painting. Spray paints present the usual difficulties, though you do get a very good over-painting effect from spray paints as the fine mist of colour is ideal to create light and shadows. Brushes are good, but do be careful about the amount of paint on the brush as too much will cause blobs of paint that will spoil the effect. A dry brush with almost no paint on it is a good starting point.

Step 1. Squeeze out excess paint after soaking the sponge in a shallow paint tray

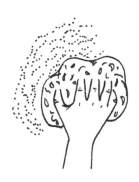

Step 2. Dab the sponge evenly and softly over the surface

Step 3. Apply a second colour when the first is dry

Sponging a background

Exciting effects are gained by stenciling over an interesting painted background, and a sponged finish is one of the simplest background treatments. It's an absolute blessing for uneven or damaged walls, as its subtle effect tends to mask any undulations. I often use it as a background for stencilling, and it can be an excellent way of combining two colours already in use in the stencil. Remember, though, that two colours sponged on together often produce a totally different colour, such as yellow ochre overlayed with red will produce an orange effect. If you're a beginner, you are better off working in shades of one colour. Choose your main deep colour and add white to give you progressively lighter shades.

Trial and error will be the best way to decide just what two, or three, colours you are going to combine in your sponging. Some experts like to use a deep base colour, overlayed with a lighter shade. Others swear by the opposite method! So, experiments are needed. I also like to do a sample piece of board and examine it in shadow, near a well-lit window, and at night and during the day. That way you will see the full effect your colour combinations will take on in all lights, or at any time of the day. Colour combinations are likely to be more affected by light than a single colour, causing them to take on variable effects.

To sponge a background you will need: a large, good quality natural sponge; acrylic, or emulsion (water-based) paints; rubber gloves; paint containers – a shallow tray will work well.

Paint your walls or item with the base coat. Several coats may be needed to give a good, opaque base. Allow each coat to dry thoroughly before applying the next one.

Your top colour may need thinning with water. Experiment with a little paint first, by diluting it into a fluid mixture. Then place your sponge into the mixture, saturate it and squeeze it until it is no longer dripping. Use a piece of scrap paper as a trial. Dab the sponge onto the paper to test for colour density, and to see just how much pressure you need to apply.

Start to apply your top coat evenly over the base

coat, using the flattest surface of the sponge, and frequently changing the direction in which you apply it, so as to avoid the same imprint being repeated over and over again. Do not twist or slide the sponge against the wall as this will result in streaks that will smear and spoil the effect.

Apply as many top coats as you desire. You will find that a reasonably large wall will be dry by the time you finish one coat, and you can get on with applying your next coat almost immediately.

If you are using sponging as an effect on it's own you can afford to be bold in your colour combinations. However, as a background to stencilling it seems to be better to err on the side of conservatism. Subtle shading behind a stencil can give a magical effect, rather than overwhelm the stencilled design. Sponging and stencilling can help overcome decorating problems, too. For example, I have sponged my bathroom walls in two shades of pale pink (to match the existing tiles installed by a previous owner), then stencilled a border above the tiles in three stronger shades of the same pink. The effect is attractive, it blends the tiles and walls together, and can make a visitor believe that the choice of tiles was quite deliberate!

Crackled paint background

The paints to produce a crackled effect are available from most craft and art supply shops. They work on the principle of the top coat of paint drying at a different surface tension to that of the base coat. A crackle medium or paint is applied over the base coat. This causes the top coat to dry crackled and crazed, revealing the colour of the base coat through the cracks of the paint. It's a very simple process, and it creates a wonderfully effective aged-looking background for stencils. I have used it on smaller items, such as the tray, and the cupboard pictured. Large areas, such as walls, could also be treated in this way, but the materials needed seem only to be packaged in small quantities and this could cause the project to be expensive.

Colour combinations

Nothing has quite as much effect on our surroundings as colour. It's easy to choose a patterned paper or fabric, because the colours are already in place and their impact is immediate. Starting from scratch is another matter! The following thoughts may help you understand colour combinations, the impact they will have, and how to recognise groups of colour. It all may sound technical, but once you understand a colour's 'ranking', you will better know how and where to use it. There are many excellent books written in detail about the theory of colour, and you may find it fascinating to learn more. The following ideas on colour are brief and will be helpful if you have to decide on colours for your stencils, especially where no other influences exist.

Colours are named universally, and some names of colours may appear quaint and old-fashioned. These names are known and understood by art supply shops, so you should not be shy about asking for colours by their proper name.

Colours are classed into three main groups:

Primary colours

blue, red and yellow

Secondary colours

purple, green and orange

Tertiary colours

olive green, rust and citron

When you mix any two of the primary colours together you produce a perfect secondary colour, which harmonises with the remaining primary.

For example:

- Red and blue mixed, produces purple, which harmonises with yellow.

- Red and yellow mixed, produces orange, which harmonises with blue.

- Blue and yellow mixed, produces green, which harmonises with red.

By mixing the secondary colours together you make the tertiary colours.

For example:

- Purple and green mixed, produces olive green.

- Orange and purple mixed, produces russet or rust.

- Green and orange mixed, produces citron or citrine.

For your own reference, colours that are mixed with white are called tints. Colours that are mixed with black are called shades.

Colours are divided into warm and cool colours. Warm colours are red, orange and yellow, the cool colours are green, blue and violet. Black and white can fit into either category, depending on the classification of nearby colours.

Projects shown on colour pages

Page 1

Stencilled Cupboard

The cupboard was first painted with a 'crackle' surface. This preparation comes under several brands, such as Weathered Wood, Crackle Glaze and others. The method relies on the second coat of paint drying at a different surface tension to the 'crackle' varnish. This causes splits and crazing, revealing the base colour. The background colours on the cupboard were completed before any stencilling was done. Areas of blue at the front were painted after masking off the area with masking tape. Masking tape will give you very straight paint lines. The whole cupboard was then sealed with a matt acrylic sealer.

Page 2

Roses

A motif from a wonderful chintz inspired these rose stencils. The watering can has been stencilled at random with roses, combining leaves and buds. The background had strips of masking tape laid down, then the spaces between were lightly sponged with soft pink. The rose swag border picks up the pinks used in the fabric.

Page 3

Stencilled memories

I first found the lovely old frame, then worked out the sizing and spacing of the sampler. I practised on paper first, being sure that the final border was narrow enough not to look squashed. This practice session also gave me an idea of the spacing needed between the letters. I first made chalk lines across the fabric to help me align the bottom of the letters. Find the centre of the fabric, and start with the centre letter in the line. Then stencil to the left and the right until the line is completed. I used a cotton homespun fabric as a base, acrylic paints (though you could use stencil crayons) and pressed the fabric on the wrong side when completed, to set the paints. The nautical motifs could easily be replaced with pretty motifs, or even those with a nursery theme.

The seaside at your feet

These pine floorboards were first limed. A watery solution of off-white acrylic paint was painted on, then immediately wiped off. This left a faint residue of paint that gave the wood a limed appearance. Various shell stencils were applied, each using soft, neutral colours. I used several tones of the same colour in each stencil to give the motifs depth.

Page 4

Nursery magic

Stencils on the old doll's cradle have picked up the designs and colours of the wall stencilling. You could also paint the rocking horse motif on fabric for curtains or a quilt (though be sure to wash fabric before stencilling), or use the motif on cupboards or a chest of drawers. The charm of these stencils is in the strong, bright colours, though paler colours may be used successfully providing they have some vibrancy.

Page 5

Stencilled writing paper and envelopes

I found some good quality recycled writing paper with a lovely texture and soft colouring. Simple stencil motifs on envelopes, notelets and on larger paper will enhance and personalise writing paper of all descriptions.

A Victorian-inspired floor stencil

Floor stencils can enhance hallways, define areas in a large room, or become a decorative substitute for rugs and carpets. Try a small motif evenly spaced over a floor, then edged with a border or two – it will look like a rug! Consider painting poor quality timber floors that have mismatched or damaged planks, then stencil over them for maximum design impact.

Page 6

Country-look stencils

Stacks of papier mache boxes, a basket and a chest have been stencilled with acrylic paints. The lids of the boxes have been sponged with colours used in the stencil designs. The noticeboard is made of hessian, and the border was simply taken as far as it could go, leaving a space for the small bird. This saved time-consuming calculations as to where the border should start and finish. The tray was treated with a 'crackle' surface first, then the roosters and border were stencilled. The upper ridge of the tray was sponged lightly with the border colour. The rim of the terracotta pot was stencilled with a section of a border. Cork place mats have the stencil motif centred, and have been painted with acrylic paints.

Page 7

Schoolhouse quilt

There are many ways of making this quilt, and I've no doubt that ardent quilters will wish to adapt it for themselves! The quilt blocks are all identical, except for colour, and they can all be different as mine are, or you may choose to use fewer colours. I have used red, blue, beige and green in acrylic paints and matched these to plain fabrics. The strips and the block bases are cut from good quality cotton homespun fabric, pre-washed and ironed. Stencil the schoolhouses first, then heat seal the paint by ironing the squares on the back, using a medium heat. Join the stencilled blocks in horizontal rows, stitching plain coloured vertical strips between them. Then stitch these completed rows to the long horizontal plain strips. Stitch the inner plain border around the quilt top, then the outer border. Sandwich a layer of quilter's batting between the quilt top and a lightweight cotton lining fabric. Hold the layers together with safety pins or basting, or both! Quilt around the edges of the stencil motifs by hand or machine, using good quality quilting thread. Place the backing fabric over the quilt top, right sides facing, and stitch around the outside, leaving an opening for turning. Turn, press lightly. Stitch through all layers at seam lines of border strips. Hang quilt, or place on bed, then stand back and admire it!

Page 8

Embroidered stencil on a silk cushion

I used DMC/Myart's stencil crayons to colour this rose motif and border. Practise first on paper to get the proportions correct. Stencil the border first, taking care to get the corners accurate, then stencil the rose in the centre of the fabric. Embroider around the flowers and leaves with small blanket stitch, using two strands of DMC embroidery cotton, to give the impression of hand sewn applique. When the embroidery is complete, place the fabric right side down on a smooth pad of fine fabric, such as lawn, on the ironing board. Pin the embroidery onto the lawn, and down into the ironing board padding. Pin all around the fabric piece, stretching it taut, and being sure it is straight and even. When no wrinkles remain, spray the whole piece lightly with starch and press the fabric. Leave the piece pinned until it has cooled, then remove it to sew into your cushion. The frill strip is folded over to make it double, and has the rose leaves stencilled to flow up from the raw edges. The piping strip was brushed with the green crayon to give piping in exactly the colour I needed.

Credits

Thank you to DMC/Myart in Sydney for their stencil crayons and brushes, and their wonderful range of embroidery threads; C & S Imports in Melbourne (Just Craft Shops in Sydney and Melbourne) for acrylic stencil paints, crackle glazes, papier mache boxes and baskets and the metal watering can; Hopscotch Toys of Lindfield for the toy yacht and wooden truck; Ray Toby fabrics in Sydney for the plain homespun fabrics in the schoolhouse quilt; and to Grosvenor Antiques, Lindfield, Sydney, for the pine duck cutlery holder on the cover.

For information about craft kits and materials available from Tonia Todman, please write to:

Tonia Todman Craft Kits
PO Box 12
Balmain NSW 2041

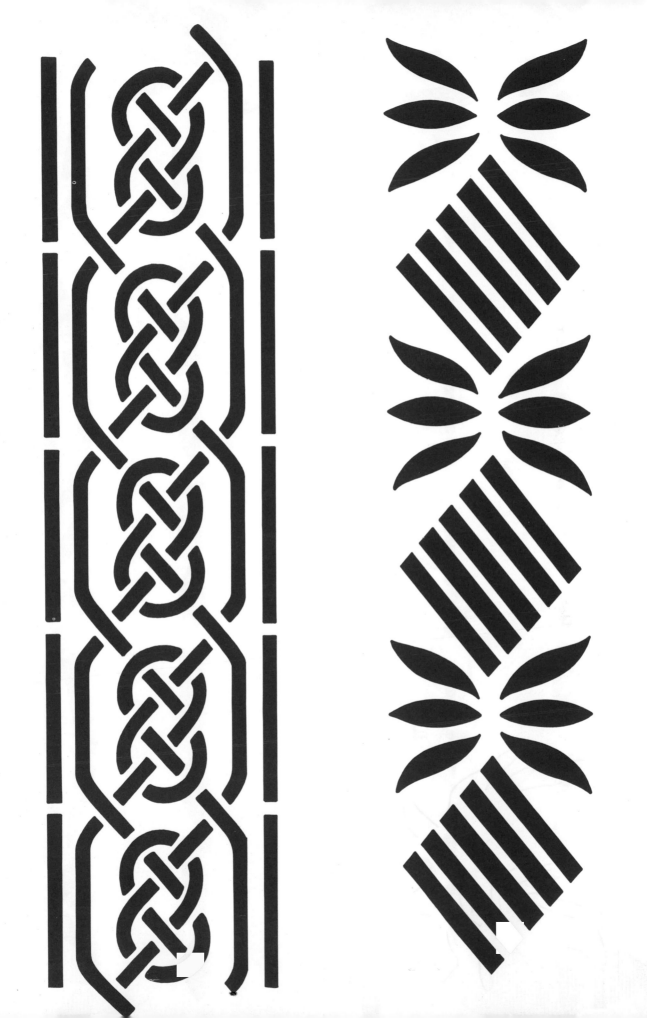

ABCDE

FGHIJK

LMNOP

QRSTU

VWXYZ

abcdefgh

ijklmnop

qrstuvw

xyz1234

567890